LES MISÉRABLES

France in the 1830s. The rich ride in carriages, and eat from gold plates. The poor have no work, no food, no hope – they are *Les Misérables*, and rebellion is in the air. France remembers the French Revolution in 1789, when the people built barricades in the streets of Paris, and the dead were counted in thousands. Is that time coming again?

This is the story of Jean Valjean. A prisoner for nineteen years, now at last he is a free man. But how can he live, where can he find work? What hope is there for a man like him? It is also the story of Javert, a police inspector, a cruel man, a hard man. He wants one thing in life – to send Valjean back to prison. And it is Fantine's story too, Fantine and her daughter Cosette. How does their story change Valjean's life? And it is also Marius's story. He is a student in Paris, ready to die for the rebellion – or for love. And last, there is Gavroche – a boy of the Paris streets, with no home, no family, no shoes . . . but a boy with a smile on his face and a song in his heart.

But we begin with Jean Valjean . . .

OXFORD BOOKWORMS LIBRARY

Human Interest

Les Misérables

Stage 1 (400 headwords)

Series Editor: Jennifer Bassett
Founder Editor: Tricia Hedge
Activities Editors: Jennifer Bassett and Christine Lindop

For Richard

RETOLD BY JENNIFER BASSETT

Les Misérables

Illustrated by
Giorgio Bacchin

OXFORD UNIVERSITY PRESS

OXFORD
UNIVERSITY PRESS

Great Clarendon Street, Oxford, OX2 6DP, United Kingdom

Oxford University Press is a department of the University of Oxford.
It furthers the University's objective of excellence in research, scholarship,
and education by publishing worldwide. Oxford is a registered trade
mark of Oxford University Press in the UK and in certain other countries

ISBN: 978 0 19 479440 4

A complete recording of this Bookworms edition of
Les Misérables is available.

Printed in China

Word count (main text): 7,302 words

For more information on the Oxford Bookworms Library,
visit www.oup.com/elt/gradedreaders

ACKNOWLEDGEMENTS

Illustrations by: Georgio Bacchin

CONTENTS

Chapter 1
Jean Valjean

🏃

FOREWORD

It is the year 1796, and the people of France are hungry. Not the rich people, of course. They have food, they have warm clothes, they have beautiful houses. No, it is the poor people of France . . .

Jean Valjean is one of these poor people. He is a young man, big, strong, and a good worker – but he has no work, he cannot find work, and he is hungry. He lives with his sister in the village of Brie. Her husband is dead, and she has seven children. It is a cold hard winter, and there is no food in the house. No bread, nothing – and seven children!

Jean Valjean is a good man, he is not a thief. But how can a man just sit there, when his sister's children cry all night because they are hungry? What can a man do?

He leaves his house at night, and goes down the village street. He puts his hand through the window of the bakery – crash! – he takes a loaf of bread, and he runs. He runs fast, but other people run faster.

France is not kind to poor people. France sends Jean Valjean to prison for five years. After four years he escapes. They find him, and bring him back. They give him six more years. Once again, he escapes, and two days later, they find him. And they give him another eight years.

Nineteen years in prison – for a loaf of bread!

In 1815, when he leaves prison, Jean Valjean is a different man. Prison changes people. Years of misery, years of back-breaking work, years of cruel prison guards. These things change a man. Once there was love in Jean Valjean's heart. Now, there is only hate.

One evening in October, in the year 1815, there was a knock on the door of the Bishop of Digne's house.

'Come in,' said the bishop. The bishop was a kind man; everyone in the town of Digne knew that. Poor people, hungry people, miserable people – they all came to the door of the bishop's house.

The bishop's sister looked at the man at the door that night, and she was afraid.

'Look at him!' she whispered to the bishop. 'He is a big man, and a dangerous one. He carries a yellow card, so he was once a prisoner – a bad man.'

But the bishop did not listen. 'Come in, my friend,' he said to the man at the door. 'Come in. You must eat dinner with us, and sleep in a warm bed tonight.'

The man stared at the bishop. 'My name is Jean Valjean,' he said. 'I was a prisoner in Toulon for nineteen years. Here is my yellow card, see? People everywhere shut their doors in my face – but not you. Why not?'

'Because, my friend, in the eyes of God you are my brother,' said the bishop, smiling. 'So, come in, and sit by our fire.' The bishop turned to his sister. 'Now, sister, our friend Jean Valjean needs a good dinner. Bring out the silver dinner plates. It's a special night tonight.'

'Not the silver plates!' whispered the bishop's sister. Her eyes went quickly to Jean Valjean, then back to the bishop's face.

'Yes, the silver plates,' said the bishop. 'And the silver candlesticks too. The church has these beautiful things, but they are for our visitors. And our visitor tonight must have only the best.'

And so Jean Valjean sat down with the bishop and his sister and ate from silver plates. He ate hungrily – it was his first good meal for weeks.

'You're a good man,' he said to the bishop. 'Perhaps the only good man in France.'

But Valjean could not take his eyes away from the silver plates. After the meal, the bishop's sister put the silver plates away, and Valjean's eyes watched. He saw the place, and he remembered it.

In the night, in his warm bed in the bishop's house, he

Valjean could not take his eyes away from the silver plates.

thought about the plates. They were big, heavy – so much silver in them! 'I can sell those plates,' he thought. 'For just one of them, I can eat well for months!'

Nineteen years in prison is a long time, and nineteen hard years change a man.

- ——— -

By morning Valjean was a long way from the bishop's house. But how do you carry big silver plates? How do you hide them? People in Digne began to whisper . . .

'Did you see him? That big man, carrying six silver plates? Where did he get them from, eh?'

'Those plates came from the church. A man like that doesn't have silver plates!'

'No! And he carries a yellow card, did you see? So he was a prisoner once. He's a thief – he stole those plates!'

The police heard the whispers. They went after Jean Valjean, found him, and took him back to the bishop's house in the afternoon. But there, they had a surprise.

'My dear friend!' the bishop said to Jean Valjean. 'I'm so pleased to see you. You forgot the candlesticks! I gave you the silver plates *and* the candlesticks, you remember? But you forgot to take the candlesticks when you left.'

'But this man is a thief!' said one of the policemen.

'No, no, of course not,' said the bishop, smiling. 'I *gave* the silver to Monsieur Valjean.'

'You mean he can go? He is free?' said the policeman.

'Of course,' the bishop said.

All this time Jean Valjean stared at the bishop, and said not one word. The policemen went away, and the Bishop of Digne went into his house and came out again with the two silver candlesticks. They were tall and heavy and beautiful. The bishop put the candlesticks into Jean Valjean's hands.

'Jean Valjean, my brother,' he said. 'You must leave your bad life behind you. This is God's silver, and I am giving it to you. With it, you can begin a new, good life. I am buying your soul for God.'

Jean Valjean left the town of Digne, with his silver plates and his silver candlesticks. Suddenly, he was a rich man, but he did not understand why.

'What's happening to me?' he thought. 'Everything is changing. How can I hate people when this bishop is so good to me? What shall I do? How shall I live?'

Prisoner Valjean did not understand anything. He sat down by the road, with his head in his hands, and cried. He cried for the first time in nineteen years.

How long did he sit there, crying? What did he do next, and where did he go? Nobody knows, but when the sun came up on a new day, he was a changed man.

Chapter 2

Fantine

⚬

Now we meet Fantine. She is young and beautiful, and in love with a man in Paris. But she has no family, and no money. For Fantine, this is the love of her life; for the man in Paris, it is just a summer of love.

Men are not kind to women. They have their fun, and then they walk away. The man in Paris goes home to his rich family, and leaves poor Fantine with a child, a little girl called Cosette. Fantine must find work, but how?

Fantine has a child but no husband, and a woman without a husband is nothing. Worse than nothing. People are not kind to a woman with a child but no husband. They turn their faces away, they close their doors, they say, 'There's no work here for a woman like *you.*'

Fantine loves her daughter dearly, but what can she do? So, in 1818, in a village near Paris, she leaves her little daughter with Monsieur and Madame Thénardier. They ask for seven francs a month. Fantine pays the money, holds her daughter in her arms for the last time, and leaves. She takes the road for her home town of Montreuil, and tears are running down her face. There is misery in her heart. Poor Fantine. Poor Cosette.

In Montreuil Fantine finds work in a factory. This is the

factory of Monsieur Madeleine, an important man in the town, and very rich. Everybody likes him, because he is a good man. He is kind to his workers, he helps people, and his factory gives many jobs to the townspeople.

But who is he, this Monsieur Madeleine? Where did he come from? He arrived in Montreuil at the end of 1815, but nobody knows his family, or anything about him.

Fantine sent money every month to the Thénardiers. They were not good people, and they used the money for their own daughters. Poor little Cosette was a hungry, dirty, unloved child. She worked all day – she cleaned the house, she carried water, she washed the clothes. But Fantine knew nothing of this, and she worked long hours to make money for Cosette.

The next year the Thénardiers asked for twelve francs a month; the year after that, they wanted fifteen francs.

Then Fantine lost her job at the factory, because the women did not like her.

'*She has a child, in a village somewhere near Paris.*'

'*Yes, and where's her husband? She doesn't have one!*'

'*We don't want that kind of woman here. She must go.*'

Fantine found work making shirts. It was hard work for little money. She was often ill, with a small dry cough.

The Thénardiers wrote again: 'Your daughter needs a warm dress for winter. Send ten francs at once.'

Fantine did not have ten francs. She thought long and hard, and went to the barber in the town. She took off her hat, and her golden hair fell down her back.

'That's beautiful hair,' said the barber.

'What can you give me for it?'

'Ten francs.'

'Then cut it off.'

She sent the money to the Thénardiers. 'My daughter's not cold now,' she thought. 'She's wearing my hair.'

Soon another letter came from the Thénardiers: 'Send one hundred francs, or Cosette must leave our house.'

A hundred francs! How can a poor woman get that kind of money? There was only one way.

One cold winter evening, outside a restaurant in the centre of Montreuil, a woman walked up and down.

There was snow on the ground, but the woman wore an evening dress, with flowers in her hair. Some young men came out of the restaurant, saw her, and began to call her bad names. They laughed and shouted, but the woman

A tall policeman arrived, and pulled Fantine away.

did not look at them. Then, one young man took some snow and put it down the back of the woman's dress.

The woman was Fantine. She gave a cry, turned, and hit the young man's face with her hands. People came to watch, laughing.

A tall policeman arrived, took the woman by the arm, and pulled her away. 'Come with me,' he said.

This policeman was Inspector Javert. He was new to Montreuil, and he was a hard man. To him, the law was the only important thing in life, and he hated criminals.

The law in France at that time was not kind to women like Fantine. Javert took Fantine to the office of police.

'You hit a man in the street, and that's a crime,' he told her. 'You're getting six months.'

'Six months in prison?' Fantine cried. 'No! I'm not a bad woman, Monsieur, please! I must work, I need the money for my little daughter. Please, please don't send me to prison!' She fell to the floor, crying.

'Take her away,' Javert said to a policeman.

'One moment, please,' said a new voice.

Everybody turned to look at the door, and there stood the good, the great Monsieur Madeleine. He was an important man in Montreuil.

'Inspector,' he said. 'I was outside the restaurant too, and I can tell you the true story. The young man began the fight, and this poor woman' – he looked at Fantine on the floor – 'must go free. She did nothing wrong.'

'The woman is a criminal,' said Javert angrily. 'She—'

'She must go free,' said Monsieur Madeleine. 'Ask the other people at the restaurant. We all saw the same thing.'

Fantine stood up slowly. She began to cough, a hard dry noise. Monsieur Madeleine took her arm gently.

'My dear child, you are not well,' he said.

Javert's cold eyes stared at Monsieur Madeleine.

'Do I know you from somewhere?' he said. 'Were you ever at Toulon?'

Monsieur Madeleine looked at him. His face did not change, but his eyes were suddenly very watchful. 'No, I don't know Toulon,' he said.

— ◆ ▬ -

Monsieur Madeleine took Fantine to the little hospital in Montreuil. She lay in bed, and coughed and coughed. Monsieur Madeleine listened to her sad story, and the next day he sent money to the Thénardiers.

'Now, you must get better,' he told Fantine. 'Cosette needs you.'

But Fantine did not get better. She was now very ill, and five days later the doctor spoke to Monsieur Madeleine.

'Does she have a child, this poor woman?' he said.

'Yes, a small daughter.'

'You must bring the child here – soon.'

Monsieur Madeleine went to sit by Fantine's bed.

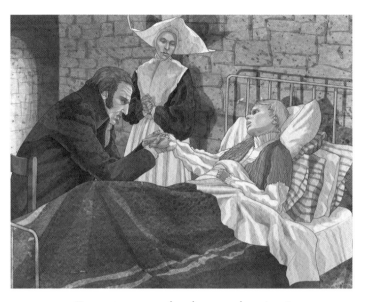

'I want to see my daughter, one last time.'

'Monsieur Madeleine' – *cough, cough* – 'you are so' – *cough, cough* – 'kind to me. I want to see my daughter, one last time. Please can you' – *cough, cough, cough* – 'bring Cosette to me? Please, Monsieur!'

Monsieur Madeleine took her hand. 'Of course I can,' he said gently, 'and then—'

The door of the room suddenly opened behind him, and Fantine cried out, 'No! No!'

Monsieur Madeleine looked round quickly. Inspector Javert came into the room, with four policemen.

'Jean Valjean, prisoner at Toulon, I am arresting you,' Javert said. 'After you left the prison, you stole money from a child in Toulon. You are still a thief, and now you must go to prison for life.'

Fantine sat up in bed. 'No!' she cried. 'Cosette . . .!'

Monsieur Madeleine stood up slowly. 'Inspector, give me three days,' he said. He was a big man, much bigger

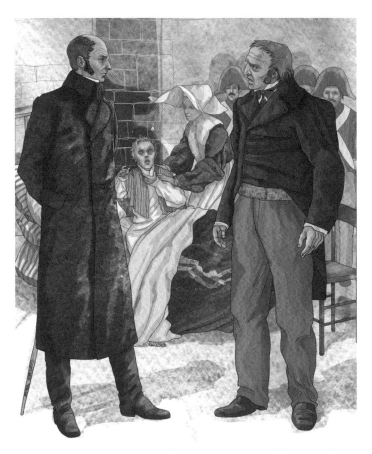

'Inspector, give me three days,' Monsieur Madeleine said.

than Javert. 'Three days, to bring this poor woman's child to her before she dies. Then you can take me.'

Javert laughed loudly. 'Three days! You're going to run away!'

Behind the two men, Fantine cried out, 'Monsieur Madeleine, please take care of Cosette, oh please . . .'

Javert turned to her. 'Be quiet, woman! There's no Monsieur Madeleine here. This man is a criminal, called Jean Valjean, and he's going to prison!'

Fantine stared at Javert, and tried to speak, but she could not. She fell back in the bed, and lay still.

She was dead.

The people of Montreuil talked about that day for a long time – the death of the woman Fantine, the arrest of Monsieur Madeleine. Javert put Monsieur Madeleine in a locked room in the police office, but in the night he broke down the door and escaped. Where did he go? Did he go to his house in the town? His old servant said no. She saw nobody, and heard nothing, she said. (She loved Monsieur Madeleine very much.)

So where did Monsieur Madeleine go? Nobody in Montreuil saw him again. One thing was certain. In Monsieur Madeleine's house there were two beautiful old silver candlesticks. The next day, they were gone.

Chapter 3

Cosette

FOREWORD

Monsieur Madeleine is, of course, Jean Valjean. You knew that already. After Digne, he sells the bishop's silver plates (but keeps the candlesticks). He comes to Montreuil, builds his factory, works hard, is kind to other people . . . He makes a new, good life, and is true to the Bishop of Digne.

But after Valjean left prison in Toulon, and before he came to Digne, he was hungry. And in a street in Toulon he stole some money from a boy. Just one franc . . . to buy bread. Because he did this, the law in France says that prisoner Valjean must go back to prison, and stay there for life. He can never be a free man again.

And so we meet Javert. Before Montreuil, he was a prison guard at Toulon. The law is his god, and he hates all criminals. He remembers Jean Valjean, that big strong man, very well. He wants to see him in prison again. And he, Inspector Javert, is going to put him there.

Jean Valjean remembers Javert now. He remembers the cold eyes, the hard voice, the cruel prison guard's smile. He remembers . . . and is afraid. He knows that Javert is his enemy for life.

But he remembers Fantine too. He remembers her dying words – *Please take care of Cosette, please* . . . How

can he leave this little girl, without a mother, without a
friend in the world? He must find her – Javert, or no Javert.

Monsieur and Madame Thénardier lived in a village
called Montfermeil near Paris. There was no water in
the village, and the nearest water was a small river in
a wood fifteen minutes' walk away. People carried the
water in buckets to their houses.

Cosette hated that wood. At night, the trees made
noises. She was frightened of the noises, frightened of
the dark, and with a heavy bucket of water, it was a long
walk home.

One dark winter night in 1823, Madame Thénardier
sent Cosette out to the river for water. Cosette ran to the
river and then, with her heavy bucket of water, she began

to walk home. The trees were noisy tonight, whispering and laughing at her, and the little girl began to cry.

'Oh please God, help me! Please, dear God!'

And suddenly, the bucket was gone. A great hand came down and took it from her. She looked up and saw a big man in an old yellow coat.

Sometimes we know, without words, when something good is happening. The little girl knew that now, and she was not frightened of the big man, not a bit.

The man spoke to her. 'Child, this is a very heavy bucket. Shall I carry it for you?'

'Yes, Monsieur.'

'How old are you?'

'I'm eight years old, Monsieur.'

'Where is your mother?'

'I don't know,' said the child. 'I haven't got a mother.'

'What's your name?'

'Cosette.'

The big man stopped. He put the bucket down and looked into Cosette's face.

'Why are you carrying a heavy bucket of water at this time of night? Who sent you?'

'Madame Thénardier.'

'I would like to talk to this Madame Thénardier. Shall we go and see her?'

'Yes, Monsieur.'

Cosette was not afraid of the tree noises now. This big

man, with his gentle voice, was a new and wonderful thing in her life. They walked to the Thénardiers' house.

'Please, Monsieur, can I carry the bucket now?'

'But why?'

A great hand came down and took the bucket from her.

'I can't ask people for help, Madame says. She hits me when I do that,' Cosette said. 'She hits me all the time.'

He gave her the bucket.

The Thénardiers were very surprised to see Cosette's new friend, this big man in the old yellow coat.

Inside the house, the big man looked at Cosette. He saw her thin clothes, her dirty hair, her big frightened eyes. She was small for her eight years. Her hands were red from kitchen work, and she had no shoes.

'Why does this child have no shoes on her feet, on this cold winter night?' he said to Madame Thénardier.

Madame Thénardier looked at Cosette angrily. 'Go into the kitchen, Cosette. There is work to do. Go!'

'And who are *you?*' Monsieur Thénardier said.

'I am here for Fantine, the child's mother,' said the big man. 'You don't need to know my name. Fantine is dead, so you can get no more money from her. Here' – he put some money on the table – 'is 1500 francs. Now call the child. I'm taking her away.'

When Jean Valjean and Cosette left Montfermeil, Cosette did not look back. She never wanted to see Madame Thénardier again.

She put her cold little hand into Valjean's great hand, and looked up into his face. 'Monsieur,' she said, 'can I . . . can I call you Father?'

Valjean looked down at her big round eyes. 'Yes,' he

said. He did not know love, he did not understand love, but in that moment, suddenly, he felt a father's love for this small child.

'Yes,' he said again. 'Yes, you can call me Father. It's a good name.'

Hand in hand, they walked away on the road to Paris.

In Paris Cosette learnt to laugh, and to sing like a bird, and to be happy. Jean Valjean learnt to be father and mother to this child, and he loved her dearly.

But they lived quietly, moved house often, and only went out at night. Because Javert, too, was in Paris. When Valjean escaped from Montreuil, Javert came to Paris to look for him. He was now an important inspector in the Paris police. Every criminal in Paris was afraid of Inspector Javert.

Once, Valjean saw Javert by the river, and the next day he looked for a new place to live. He found one, behind the high walls of a girls' school. The school gave Valjean a job as a gardener, and he lived in a little house in the big gardens. Cosette lived in the school. But every day she came to the gardener's little house for one hour. They talked, and they sang, and they read books. It was the happiest hour in the day for her and for Jean Valjean.

And so the years passed.

Chapter 4

Marius

Nine years pass. Valjean and Cosette are living in the Rue Plumet in Paris, in a house with a big garden. It is a quiet street and nobody comes there. This pleases Valjean, because he is still afraid of Inspector Javert.

Cosette is now a young woman. She is tall, with golden-brown hair. She is beautiful, but there are many beautiful faces in the world. The wonderful thing about Cosette's face is her smile – a slow, warm, gentle smile, like sunlight after rain.

And now we must meet Marius, and his young friend Gavroche. Marius is a student, a young man with many ideas but no money. Paris is full of young men like this. Marius has a grandfather (his father is dead), but he does not talk to him. Their political ideas are very different. At seventeen, he leaves home with 30 francs, his watch, and a small bag of clothes. Now, five years older, he lives with other students, and they talk all night about books and ideas, politics and government, life and death. All students are like this. They live for ideas, and do a little work here and there. When they need to.

Gavroche is a child of the Paris streets. He is eleven or twelve years old, and wears a man's trousers and a woman's shirt (a kind woman gave these clothes to him). He lives on the streets, knows everybody, goes everywhere, and enjoys life. Well, why not? He knows no other life, only this one.

Marius loved walking through the streets and gardens of Paris, and he often walked in the Luxembourg garden. One day in the garden he saw a man with a young girl. The man was about sixty, and the girl, Marius thought, was about seventeen. He did not see her eyes, but he saw her golden-brown hair and her slow gentle smile.

He walked past them once, and did not look back. But he came to the Luxembourg the next day, and the day after that, and for the next five days. The man and the girl were always there. He could not stop looking at the girl. He wanted very much to see that smile again.

On the seventh day the girl turned her head and looked at Marius. She looked into his eyes across the garden, and that look went, like a bullet from a gun, into Marius's heart. There were no words, but at once Marius knew and the girl knew. *This* was love.

Life stopped for Marius then. He spent hours in the Luxembourg, and every time he saw her, the sun came out and all the birds in the garden began singing.

But the man began to look at Marius too, and his face was not friendly. Marius was afraid, and he went to Gavroche.

'Gavroche, please, you must help me.'

'Why? What's the matter, Monsieur Marius?'

'There's a girl, Gavroche. She walks in the Luxembourg every day. I want you to follow her home and tell me the address.'

'Why don't *you* follow her? I'm busy,' said Gavroche.

'I'm afraid to,' said Marius. 'Her father, grandfather, I don't know, is watching me. He doesn't like me.'

'Why is this important, Monsieur Marius?' Gavroche said. He had a big smile on his face.

'Because I'm IN LOVE,' shouted Marius. 'Please, Gavroche, do it!'

Gavroche ran away, laughing. Two days later he came to Marius's rooms.

'Why is this important, Monsieur Marius?' asked Gavroche.

'Rue Plumet,' he said. 'House at the end of the street. Hard to find. You need to look for it.'

Spring came, and Cosette began to go out into the garden at Rue Plumet. She was usually alone. Her old servant,

Toussaint, was always in the kitchen, and Father (Jean Valjean) was in his room, reading.

Cosette was sad. She remembered the young man in the Luxembourg garden, but Father no longer wanted to go there. But that evening in the Rue Plumet garden, something very wonderful happened.

She heard a voice, a man's voice. She looked round, and it was him.

'I'm so sorry,' he said. 'Please don't be afraid. I just wanted to . . . You remember the Luxembourg garden? I saw you there for the first time . . . I can't forget you, day and night I think about you . . . Please don't be afraid . . . You see, I love you . . . It just happened to me . . . I can't stop it . . . Don't be afraid . . . please.'

Cosette listened to this wonderful river of words, and then held out her hand to him. He took her hand, and she pulled it to her, and put it against her heart.

'Then – you love me?' he said.

'Of course! You know that.'

A kiss. No words. They did not need words. Later, words came. The story of his life, the story of her life, everything. Between lovers, everything is interesting.

When they were done with words, Cosette put her head on Marius's shoulder and asked:

'What is your name?'

'My name is Marius. And yours?'

'Cosette.'

Every evening they met secretly in the garden at Rue Plumet. A kiss, a gentle laugh, whispered words of love – it was the spring and summer of their young lives.

It was the spring and summer of their young lives.

But around them, outside their garden, there was change. There were angry people; there were police and soldiers on the streets of Paris. And one day Jean Valjean said to Cosette, 'My dearest child, we live in dangerous times. We must leave France and go to England.'

Cosette looked at him with frightened eyes. 'Must we go, Father?' she said.

Valjean watched her face. 'We must,' he said. 'Get ready to leave very soon.'

There was a change in Cosette. Valjean remembered the young man in the Luxembourg garden, and he looked at Cosette's beautiful young face. He was afraid – afraid of losing his dear daughter.

That evening in the Rue Plumet garden, there were many unhappy tears.

'But you must follow us to England,' cried Cosette.

'How can I do that?' cried Marius. 'I have no money, no passport even! England to me is like the moon!'

They held hands in the moonlight.

'Listen. I have an idea,' Marius said slowly. 'Wait two days. Perhaps . . .'

'Two days?' cried Cosette. 'How can I live two days without you?'

Chapter 5

Love and Rebellion

FOREWORD

So, what is Marius's idea? It is this . . . He wants to marry Cosette, but he has no money. His grandfather has money. He must ask his grandfather . . . But his grandfather is an old man, and old men's ideas do not change easily. He shouts at Marius, Marius shouts back, and that is the end of that. The next evening he goes as usual to the Rue Plumet. There is nobody in the garden, the house is dark, the windows are closed – Cosette and her father are gone.

Marius cannot live without Cosette. He wants to die, but Gavroche tells him that his friends need him. It is June 1832, and students and workers are running through the streets of Paris, bringing rebellion to the city, and everyone must fight the government. Marius is soon at the barricades, with a gun in his hand. He is happy. Death can come at any moment with a bullet from a soldier's gun.

These are dangerous times. Jean Valjean sees Inspector Javert in a street near the Rue Plumet. What is he doing there? Are the police watching his house? Valjean does not wait. The same night he and Cosette leave Rue Plumet. They move to 7 Rue de l'Homme-Armé, and begin to get ready for England.

How can love find a way in these troubled times?

When the soldiers attacked in front of the Arsenal building, the people turned and ran, this way and that way, through the streets of the city. Marius and his friends came to the Rue de la Chanvrerie and they built their barricade there. It was two metres high, made of wood and stone. Behind their barricade, the rebels waited for the soldiers. Night came, but nothing happened.

Enjolras was the leader of the students. He called Gavroche to him.

'You're small,' he said. 'Nobody sees you. Go and have a look round the city, and then bring us any news.'

Just after midnight, Gavroche was back. 'The soldiers aren't moving,' he said. 'But there are a lot of them.' He stopped suddenly and whispered, 'Hey, who's that? That tall man, over there?'

Enjolras and Marius turned to look.

'I don't know him,' said Marius.

'People are coming and going all night,' said Enjolras. 'Why, Gavroche? Do you know him?'

'Yes,' whispered Gavroche. 'He's not one of us. He's a spy, a police spy. Name of Javert. He stopped me once, down by the river. Put me in prison all night.'

'Are you certain about this, Gavroche?' said Marius.

'I'm certain, all right,' said Gavroche. 'He's a spy!'

The rebels did not like spies. Four of Enjolras's men jumped on Javert, pulled him into the tavern behind the barricade, and tied him to the wall.

'Do we shoot him now?' asked one of the men.

'Later,' said Enjolras. 'He can wait.'

They went back outside to the barricade and listened for the sound of soldiers. Gavroche found Marius at the far end of the barricade.

'Marius,' he whispered, 'on my way back here I came past your rooms and went in.'

'Why?' whispered Marius.

'I was hungry,' said Gavroche. 'The woman in your house is nice – she always gives me something to eat. But she had a letter for you. She gave it to me. It came two days ago, she said.'

'A letter? A letter from whom?' Suddenly there was hope in Marius's heart. 'Quick – give it to me.'

The letter was from Cosette.

My dearest, Father says we must leave at once. We go tonight to 7 Rue de l'Homme-Armé, and soon to England. Oh my dear, how can I live without you? Cosette

Marius read this letter four times and then kissed it. She still loved him! He must write back to her and say his last goodbye. There was still no sound of soldiers in the street. He found some paper and a pencil.

'I want you to put this letter into Cosette's hands.'

Cosette, dearest. I came to the Rue Plumet, but you were gone already. We cannot marry. I went to my grandfather, and he said no. I have no money, and you have no money. I love you. I can never forget you. The fighting begins here very soon. When I am dead, don't be sad. Our love was beautiful. Marius

He called to Gavroche. 'I want you to take this letter to the Rue de l'Homme-Armé. Can you do that for me?'

'Yes, but not now!' said Gavroche. 'I'm staying here for the fighting. I can shoot too, you know!'

'Gavroche, you're just a boy! We don't want you to die in the fighting. Stay away from the shooting! And this letter is very important to me. It must go now. I want you to put it into Cosette's hands. Please, Gavroche.'

'Oh, very well,' said Gavroche. He took the letter, put it inside his shirt, and ran off into the dark.

When Valjean and Cosette left the house in Rue Plumet, Cosette was very sad. Valjean saw this, but he said nothing. In the Rue de l'Homme-Armé, Cosette stayed in her bedroom. Toussaint took her meals up to her.

In the night Valjean could not sleep. The city was quiet, but for how long? He went outside the house and stood in the street, listening. There were voices in the next street, and then he heard singing. A boy, singing.

Gavroche came up the street, looking at the house numbers. He saw Valjean and stopped.

'Well, young man, what's the news?' said Valjean.

'The news is that I'm hungry,' said Gavroche.

Valjean put his hand in his pocket and found a five-franc piece. Gavroche stared at it. He didn't see many five-franc pieces, and he was very pleased to see this one. He put it in his pocket.

'You're all right,' he said. 'Do you live in this street? Do you know number seven?'

'What do you want with number seven?' said Valjean.

'Letter for someone,' said Gavroche. 'A woman.'

Valjean stared at him. He felt cold. A woman. Cosette? He remembered at once the young man in the Luxembourg. He tried to smile. 'Ah, that's the letter for Cosette,' he said. 'I'm waiting for it.'

'Yes, that's her. Well, here you are,' said Gavroche. 'It comes from the barricade in the Rue de la Chanvrerie. I'm going back there now. Goodnight, Monsieur.'

Jean Valjean went back into the house with Marius's letter. He read it quickly . . . *I love you. I can never forget you* . . . So, Cosette, his dear, dear daughter, was in love. She was his world; without her, his life was nothing. He could not even think about it . . . *When I am dead, don't be sad* . . . Those words gave him hope. So the young man was one of the rebels at the barricade.

'When the soldiers start shooting,' he thought, 'that's the end of all the rebels. I do nothing, I say nothing, I keep this letter, and *poof!* Nothing changes in our lives.'

But Valjean did not feel easy. He remembered all their happy years as father and daughter, and he saw again Cosette's sad eyes when they left the Rue Plumet. How could he take her away to England?

He turned and went out of the room. A little later, he left the house, wearing dark clothes and carrying a gun, and walked away down the street.

'What do you want with number seven?' said Valjean.

Chapter 6

The Barricades

FOREWORD

It is a long night at the barricade in the Rue de la Chanvrerie. The news is bad. More and more soldiers are arriving in the city, but the people stay in their homes. This time they don't want to fight the government. Only the students are still at the barricades, waiting for the soldiers' bullets – and death.

Then a new man arrives at the barricade, a big man in dark clothes. Marius stares. It is Cosette's father, he is certain. Is he a friend or an enemy? Who knows?

Inside the tavern, Javert too waits for death. Rebels shoot spies, he knows that. Does he think about his life, waiting there in the tavern? Is the law always right? Can a criminal change and be a good man? Does Javert ask these questions? Who knows?

Daylight comes, and the shooting begins. *Ratatat-ratatat-ratatat* on the barricade, noise and shouting, cries and screams. Valjean saves Enjolras's life. Two men die. Valjean carries the bodies into the tavern, sees Javert. And Javert sees him. Then the shooting stops.

The rebels need more bullets, and Gavroche runs out to the front of the barricade. *Come back, Gavroche!* He doesn't listen, and starts singing. There are dead soldiers lying in the street. Gavroche takes the bullets from their bags and puts them into his bag. He is small and quick, and his bag is nearly full before the soldiers start shooting at him. *Come back, Gavroche!* He sings louder, but the fifth bullet hits him, and he falls down in the street. He moves once, then falls back. Gavroche is dead. A child of the Paris streets, his singing now stopped for ever, just another dead body in the rebellion.

Smoke from the guns is everywhere, it is hard to see anything. But Marius runs out into the street, picks Gavroche up, and runs back. He puts the small body on a table in the tavern, and cries.

It is going to be a long day.

Behind the barricade Enjolras talked to the men. 'They're going to attack again soon – sixty soldiers to every one of us. Marius and I are your two leaders. Gavroche brought us bullets, so let's use them well, and fight to the end.'

'Let's kill the spy now,' said one of the men.

Then Valjean spoke. 'Give him to me. I can do that for you. I'd like to shoot him.'

Enjolras looked at him. 'You saved my life, friend. You can have the spy.'

Valjean took Javert out of the tavern to a little street behind. He took out a knife.

'Oh, a knife!' said Javert. 'Of course, a criminal's way to kill. So, kill me, and be quick.'

Valjean said nothing. He cut the ropes around Javert's arms and legs, then stood up, and said:

'You're free to go.'

Javert stared. He could not understand this.

'I live in the Rue de l'Homme-Armé,' Valjean said. 'The next time we meet, you can arrest me. Now, go!'

Javert turned and walked away. Valjean fired his gun into the air, then went back to the barricade. 'It's done,' he told Enjolras.

Now the second attack began. The government had more men, more guns, more bullets – and one by one, the students began to die. Marius was on top of the barricade. He was one of the last men still alive, but then one, two bullets hit him, and he fell. Two great hands at

'You're free to go,' said Valjean.

once picked him up. 'Cosette,' whispered Marius, and then he went into that dark night.

Jean Valjean knew Paris well, knew its little back streets, its secret places. He used them now. With the dead or dying Marius in his arms, he ran through the back streets, watching at every corner. Night came, and the sky was full of the smoke from the guns. Valjean stopped to rest. In Marius's pocket he found a piece of paper.

Take my body to my grandfather's house in . . .

The address was in the Marais, not far away. Valjean began to pick up Marius's body again – and a hand came down hard on his shoulder. Valjean turned.

Javert stood behind him. 'What are you doing here?' he said. 'Who is this man?'

Valjean stood up. 'Inspector Javert,' he said, 'I told you, I'm tired of running and hiding. You can arrest me, put me back in prison. I ask just one thing. Help me to take this young man home. That is all.'

'He's dead,' said Javert.

'No. Not yet. He lives in the Marais with his grand-father. Look.' He showed Javert the piece of paper.

Javert read the address, then called to a carriage along the street. They put Marius's body on the back seat, and sat side by side on the front seat.

At the house of Marius's grandfather, a servant opened the door. She gave a little scream when she saw Marius in Valjean's arms. 'It's Monsieur Marius!'

'Take the boy in,' said Javert. 'I'm waiting for you here at the door.' His voice was different, uncertain.

A hand came down hard on Valjean's shoulder.

Valjean looked at him, then carried Marius's body into the house. 'Call a doctor quickly,' he said to the servants. 'He was at the barricade and has two bullets still in him.' Then he came back downstairs and out into the street.

Javert was gone. Valjean looked up and down the street. Nothing. Nobody.

Down by the river Seine, near the Place du Châtelet, Javert stood on the bridge, looking down into the water.

'What must I do?' he thought, but for the first time in his life he had no answer. Valjean's words at the barricade went through his head again and again. *You're free to go . . . free to go . . . free to go.*

'I can do one of two things,' Javert said to the river. 'I can arrest him, or I can *not* arrest him and say "You are free to go." But the law is the law – so I must arrest him. But he gave me my life – so I must give him *his* life. But the law is the law . . .'

And a voice in Javert's head said, *You worked for the law all your life, but Jean Valjean is a better man than you are.*

For a long time Javert stared down at the river, but the river gave him no answer to his question. Then he took off his hat, and put it carefully on the ground. A moment later, he stood high on the bridge, then fell, down into the dark river.

There was a splash, and that was all.

Chapter 7

Love and Death

FOREWORD

Marius lies for a long time between life and death, but months later, he is well again. Cosette visits him every day, and this of course helps him a lot. His grandfather is happy to have his grandson back, and is happy to have a new granddaughter in Cosette. The two young people marry, and live in the house of Marius's grandfather in the Marais.

There is a surprise for the young people. Cosette has money, a lot of money, Valjean tells them. She has six hundred thousand francs. This pleases Marius's grandfather very much, but the young people are only interested in love, not in money.

Where does it come from, this money? Years ago, when Valjean was Monsieur Madeleine with a factory, he was a rich man. Before he left Montreuil, he took his money and the bishop's candlesticks to a secret place. When he needs money, he goes back there.

Now this money is for Cosette, and the candlesticks stand in Valjean's house in the Rue de l'Homme-Armé. They look very fine, and Toussaint cleans them every day.

A new life begins for everybody, but there are still secrets from the past, and Valjean wants to tell them. He feels old and tired. Death is coming for him at last, he feels. He calls Cosette and Marius to his bedside.

'Listen, dearest Cosette, to the story of your mother,' he says. Cosette hears the story of Fantine's sad life. She learns that Valjean is not her real father, but in her life there is only one father, and that is Valjean, she tells him.

'Come closer, my children,' he says. 'I love you dearly, and I die happy. Come closer, and take my hands.'

Cosette and Marius are by his bed, holding his hands and crying. His great hands are still, and do not move again. He lies with his head turned up to the sky, and the light from the bishop's candlesticks falls upon his face.

GLOSSARY

arrest to take somebody to a police station for questioning

attack to start fighting or hurting somebody

bakery a bread shop

barber a barber cuts people's hair

barricade things put across a road, to stop people getting past

bishop an important priest in the Christian church

bullet a small piece of metal that comes out of a gun

carriage a kind of 'car', pulled by horses

certain sure about something

cough to send air out of the throat with a sudden loud noise

crime something that somebody does that is against the law

criminal a person who does something that is against the law

cruel very unkind

escape to get free from a place

factory a building where people make things

foreword a short introduction, telling the reader what is going
  to happen next

franc French money

frightened very afraid

fun a good time; something you enjoy

gentle quiet and kind

gone *(adj)* not there; away from a place

government the group of people who control a country

guard *(n)* a person who stops somebody from escaping

hate strong feeling of not liking; opposite of love

heart the place inside you where your feelings are

heavy difficult to lift or move

idea a plan or thought in your head

inspector a police officer

job   the work that people do for money

kiss *(v & n)*   to touch someone lovingly with your mouth

law (**the law**)   all the rules of a country

leader   a person who controls a group of people

Madame / Monsieur   French for Mrs / Mr

miserable *(adj)*   very unhappy; **misery** *(n)*   great unhappiness

    Les Misérables   French for unhappy poor people

politics   the work and ideas of government; **political** *(adj)*

prison   a place where criminals must stay as a punishment

rebel   a person who fights against the government

rebellion   a time of fighting against the government of a country

rope   very thick strong string

sad   not happy

save   to take somebody away from danger

secret   something that other people do not know about

servant   a person who works in another person's house

shoot   to fire a gun

silver   a shiny grey metal that is valuable

snow   soft white pieces of frozen water that fall from the sky

soul   the part of a person that some people believe does not die

spy   a person who tries to learn secrets about other people

stare   to look at somebody or something for a long time

steal (past tense **stole**)   to secretly take something that is not yours

surprise   something that you did not know and did not expect

take care of   to do what is necessary for someone; to look after

tavern *(old use)*   a place where people go to drink; a pub

tear *(n)*   water that comes from your eyes when you cry

thief   a person who steals something

tie *(v)*   to fasten or fix something using rope, string, etc.

troubled *(adj)*   worrying; having a lot of problems

whisper   to speak very, very quietly

wood   a big group of trees

ACTIVITIES

Before Reading

1 **Read the back cover of the book, and the introduction on the first page. How much do you know now about the story? Tick one box for each sentence.**

                                                    YES NO

1 Jean Valjean was in prison for nineteen years. ☐   ☐
2 Javert wants to help Valjean in his new life. ☐   ☐
3 The poor people in France are unhappy.   ☐   ☐
4 Fantine has a son called Marius.   ☐   ☐
5 Life is easy for everyone in France in 1815.   ☐   ☐
6 Gavroche lives with his mother and father.   ☐   ☐
7 In the French Revolution there were
   barricades in the streets of Paris.   ☐   ☐

2 **What is going to happen to the people in this story? Can you guess? Choose words to complete these sentences.**

1 Jean Valjean *marries / does not marry* Fantine.
2 Inspector Javert *sends / does not send* Jean Valjean back to prison.
3 By the end of the story Jean Valjean is *very rich / still poor*.
4 *Marius / Gavroche* dies in the rebellion.
5 Fantine dies when she is *very old / still young*.
6 When she is a young woman, Cosette has a *happy / sad* life.

48

ACTIVITIES

After Reading

1 **Who is who in this story? Choose a name to complete the first parts of the sentences. Then match the two parts of sentences together, and choose the best linking word.**

Bishop of Digne / Cosette / Fantine / Gavroche / Javert /
Jean Valjean / Marius / Monsieur Madeleine / Thénardiers

First parts of sentences

1 _____ hated all criminals, . . .

2 _____ wanted to marry Cosette very much, . . .

3 _____ had a factory in Montreuil, . . .

4 The _____ often helped poor, hungry people, . . .

5 _____ never knew her mother . . .

6 _____ wanted to take care of Fantine's daughter, . . .

7 The _____ were not kind to little Cosette, . . .

8 _____ was a child, only eleven or twelve years old, . . .

9 _____ cut off her hair and sold it . . .

Second parts of sentences

10 *so / because* she lived with the Thénardier family.

11 *when / before* a soldier shot him and killed him.

12 *but / so* he went to his grandfather and asked for money.

13 *and / but* he gave Valjean dinner and a bed for the night.

14 *but / and* he wanted to put Valjean in prison again.

15 *and / but* they asked Fantine for more money all the time.

16 *because / but* she wanted her daughter to have a warm
   dress for winter.

17 *because / so* he took her away from the Thénardiers.

18 *so / but* people in that town knew nothing about him.

2 **Here are three people from the story talking or writing to
someone. Complete the passages with words from this list
(one word for each gap). Then say who is speaking or
writing, and to whom.**

*asking, cold, daughter, dress, family, five, francs, girl,
grandfather, hands, know, letter, marry, No, nothing,
took, warm*

1 'Why are you here? You only come to see your poor
   old _____ when you want something. And now you're
   _____ for money because you want to _____ someone.
   Who is this _____? What's her _____ ? You know _____
   about her. Well, young man, the answer is "_____ "!'

2 'I don't want my _____ to be _____ in the winter, so I
   am sending you ten _____. Please buy Cosette a new
   _____ with this money – something nice and _____ .'

3 'Yes, I _____ the letter to number seven. No, I didn't put
   it into her _____, I gave it to a man. No, I don't _____
   his name, but he knew all about it. He said, "Ah, that's
   the _____ for Cosette." He was all right – he gave me
   _____ francs. That's a lot of money!'

3 Complete this crossword with words from the story, using the clues below to help you.

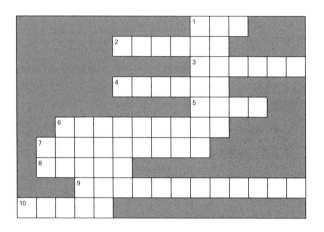

1 Gavroche told Marius that Javert was a police _____.

2 A _____ cut off Fantine's hair and paid her ten francs.

3 The bishop's candlesticks were made of _____.

4 Jean Valjean stole some _____ from the bishop.

5 Marius fell in _____ with Cosette.

6 A _____ is when people fight against the government of a country.

7 The students built a _____ in the street.

8 The Thénardiers were very _____ to little Cosette.

9 The bishop gave the two _____ to Jean Valjean.

10 Javert knew Jean Valjean because he was a _____ at the prison in Toulon when Valjean was there.

4 There are two hidden words in the crossword above. What are they? Use them to make a sentence about Jean Valjean.

5 **Here is the conversation between Marius and Cosette when Marius first opens his eyes in his grandfather's house. Put their conversation in the right order, and write in the speakers' names. Cosette speaks first (number 3).**

1 _____ 'He doesn't hate you. He loves you very much. He likes me too! And he wants me to be his granddaughter!'

2 _____ 'That's the best news of my life! Kiss me, Cosette!'

3 *Cosette* 'Oh, Marius! How are you feeling, my dearest?'

4 _____ 'Granddaughter? You mean – we can get married?'

5 _____ 'You're in your grandfather's house.'

6 _____ 'I'm . . . I'm all right, I think. But where am I?'

7 _____ 'Of course not! You can have a kiss when you're better – and not before!'

8 _____ 'My grandfather! Why? How? He hates me!'

9 _____ 'Yes, Marius, we can. Isn't that wonderful?'

6 **What did you think about the people in this story? Choose some names, and finish the sentences in your own words.**

Bishop of Digne / Cosette / Fantine / Gavroche / Javert / Jean Valjean / Marius / Monsieur Madeleine / the Thénardiers

1 I felt sorry for _____ because _____.

2 I liked _____ because _____.

3 I was angry with _____ when _____.

4 _____ was right to _____.

5 _____ was wrong to _____.

ABOUT THE AUTHOR AND THE STORY

Jennifer Bassett has worked in English Language Teaching since 1972, and has been a teacher, teacher trainer, editor, and materials writer. She is the Series Editor of the *Oxford Bookworms Library*, and has written over twenty original and retold stories for the series, including *The Phantom of the Opera*, *One-Way Ticket*, *The President's Murderer*, *The Omega Files*, *Shirley Homes and the Lithuanian Case*, all at Stage 1, and *William Shakespeare* at Stage 2.

Her adaptations *Rabbit-Proof Fence* (Stage 3) and *Love Among the Haystacks* (Stage 2) won Language Learner Literature Awards from the Extensive Reading Foundation. Five other titles have been finalists for the Awards <www.erfoundation. com>. She has also created a new sub-series called *Bookworms World Stories*, which are collections of short stories written in English from around the world. With H. G. Widdowson, she is series co-adviser of the *Oxford Bookworms Collection*, volumes of unadapted short stories for advanced learners. Jennifer lives and works in Devonshire, in south-west England.

The story of *Les Misérables* is known all around the world. First, there was the famous novel, published in 1862, by the great French writer Victor Hugo. It is more than 1200 pages long and has a huge number of characters. The first film adaptation was made in 1907, and since then there have been more than fifty films made for cinema and television. Most famously, there is the musical, *Les Misérables* (which is often called *Les Mis*). This opened in London, England, in 1985, and is now the longest-running musical in the world. It has played in 42 countries, in 21 different languages, and to more than 57 million people!

OXFORD BOOKWORMS LIBRARY

Classics • Crime & Mystery • Factfiles • Fantasy & Horror
Human Interest • Playscripts • Thriller & Adventure
True Stories • World Stories

The OXFORD BOOKWORMS LIBRARY provides enjoyable reading in English, with a wide range of classic and modern fiction, non-fiction, and plays. It includes original and adapted texts in seven carefully graded language stages, which take learners from beginner to advanced level. An overview is given on the next pages.

All Stage 1 titles are available as audio recordings, as well as over eighty other titles from Starter to Stage 6. All Starters and many titles at Stages 1 to 4 are specially recommended for younger learners. Every Bookworm is illustrated, and Starters and Factfiles have full-colour illustrations.

The OXFORD BOOKWORMS LIBRARY also offers extensive support. Each book contains an introduction to the story, notes about the author, a glossary, and activities. Additional resources include tests and worksheets, and answers for these and for the activities in the books. There is advice on running a class library, using audio recordings, and the many ways of using Oxford Bookworms in reading programmes. Resource materials are available on the website <www.oup.com/elt/gradedreaders>.

The *Oxford Bookworms Collection* is a series for advanced learners. It consists of volumes of short stories by well-known authors, both classic and modern. Texts are not abridged or adapted in any way, but carefully selected to be accessible to the advanced student.

You can find details and a full list of titles in the *Oxford Bookworms Library Catalogue* and *Oxford English Language Teaching Catalogues*, and on the website <www.oup.com/elt/gradedreaders>.

THE OXFORD BOOKWORMS LIBRARY
GRADING AND SAMPLE EXTRACTS

STARTER • 250 HEADWORDS
present simple – present continuous – imperative –
can/cannot, must – going to (future) – simple gerunds …

Her phone is ringing – but where is it?

Sally gets out of bed and looks in her bag. No phone. She looks under the bed. No phone. Then she looks behind the door. There is her phone. Sally picks up her phone and answers it. *Sally's Phone*

STAGE 1 • 400 HEADWORDS
… past simple – coordination with *and, but, or* –
subordination with *before, after, when, because, so* …

I knew him in Persia. He was a famous builder and I worked with him there. For a time I was his friend, but not for long. When he came to Paris, I came after him – I wanted to watch him. He was a very clever, very dangerous man. *The Phantom of the Opera*

STAGE 2 • 700 HEADWORDS
… present perfect – *will* (future) – (*don't*) *have to, must not, could* –
comparison of adjectives – simple *if* clauses – past continuous –
tag questions – *ask/tell* + infinitive …

While I was writing these words in my diary, I decided what to do. I must try to escape. I shall try to get down the wall outside. The window is high above the ground, but I have to try. I shall take some of the gold with me – if I escape, perhaps it will be helpful later. *Dracula*

STAGE 3 • 1000 HEADWORDS

... should, *may* – present perfect continuous – *used to* – past perfect –
causative – relative clauses – indirect statements ...

Of course, it was most important that no one should see Colin, Mary, or Dickon entering the secret garden. So Colin gave orders to the gardeners that they must all keep away from that part of the garden in future. *The Secret Garden*

STAGE 4 • 1400 HEADWORDS

... past perfect continuous – passive (simple forms) –
would conditional clauses – indirect questions –
relatives with *where*/*when* – gerunds after prepositions/phrases ...

I was glad. Now Hyde could not show his face to the world again. If he did, every honest man in London would be proud to report him to the police. *Dr Jekyll and Mr Hyde*

STAGE 5 • 1800 HEADWORDS

... future continuous – future perfect –
passive (modals, continuous forms) –
would have conditional clauses – modals + perfect infinitive ...

If he had spoken Estella's name, I would have hit him. I was so angry with him, and so depressed about my future, that I could not eat the breakfast. Instead I went straight to the old house.
Great Expectations

STAGE 6 • 2500 HEADWORDS

... passive (infinitives, gerunds) – advanced modal meanings –
clauses of concession, condition

When I stepped up to the piano, I was confident. It was as if I knew that the prodigy side of me really did exist. And when I started to play, I was so caught up in how lovely I looked that I didn't worry how I would sound. *The Joy Luck Club*

BOOKWORMS · FANTASY & HORROR · STAGE 1

The Phantom of the Opera

JENNIFER BASSETT

It is 1880, in the Opera House in Paris. Everybody is talking about the Phantom of the Opera, the ghost that lives somewhere under the Opera House. The Phantom is a man in black clothes. He is a body without a head, he is a head without a body. He has a yellow face, he has no nose, he has black holes for eyes. Everybody is afraid of the Phantom – the singers, the dancers, the directors, the stage workers . . .

But who has actually seen him?

BOOKWORMS · TRUE STORIES · STAGE 1

Ned Kelly: A True Story

CHRISTINE LINDOP

When he was a boy, he was poor and hungry. When he was a young man, he was still poor and hungry. He learnt how to steal horses, he learnt how to fight, he learnt how to live – outside the law. Australia in the 1870s was a hard, wild place. Rich people had land, poor people didn't. So the rich got richer, and the poor stayed poor.

Some say Ned Kelly was a bad man. Some say he was a good man but the law was bad. This is the true story of Australia's most famous outlaw.